W9-AVM-351

Minnesota Wild

Taylor Reed

www.av2books.com

AV² provides enriched content that supplements and complements this book. Weigl's AV² books strive to create inspired learning and engage young minds in a total learning experience.

Your AV² Media Enhanced books come alive with...

Audio
Listen to sections of the book read aloud.

Key Words
Study vocabulary, and complete a matching word activity.

Video
Watch informative video clips.

Quizzes
Test your knowledge.

Embedded Weblinks
Gain additional information for research.

Slide Show
View images and captions, and prepare a presentation.

Try This!
Complete activities and hands-on experiments.

... and much, much more!

Go to **www.av2books.com**, and enter this book's unique code.

BOOK CODE

B 5 7 4 3 2 9

AV² by Weigl brings you media enhanced books that support active learning.

Published by AV² by Weigl
350 5th Avenue, 59th Floor
New York, NY 10118
Websites: www.av2books.com   www.weigl.com

Copyright © 2016 AV² by Weigl
All rights reserved. No part of this publication may be reproduced, stored in a retrieval system, or transmitted in any form or by any means, electronic, mechanical, photocopying, recording, or otherwise, without the prior written permission of the publisher.

Library of Congress Control Number: 2014951940

ISBN 978-1-4896-3149-7 (hardcover)
ISBN 978-1-4896-3150-3 (single-user eBook)
ISBN 978-1-4896-3151-0 (multi-user eBook)

Printed in the United States of America in Brainerd, Minnesota
1 2 3 4 5 6 7 8 9 0   19 18 17 16 15

032015
WEP050315

Senior Editor Heather Kissock
Art Director Terry Paulhus

Photo Credits
Every reasonable effort has been made to trace ownership and to obtain permission to reprint copyright material. The publishers would be pleased to have any errors or omissions brought to their attention so that they may be corrected in subsequent printings.

Weigl acknowledges Getty Images and iStock as its primary image suppliers for this title.

Minnesota Wild

CONTENTS

Introduction

The Minnesota Wild is a National Hockey League (NHL) team based in St. Paul, Minnesota. Beginning with its opening season in 2000, the Wild was the first team in Minnesota since the North Stars departed to Dallas in 1993. The Wild is the only professional sports **franchise** in Minnesota to play in St. Paul. The other three teams, the Minnesota Timberwolves, Vikings, and Twins, play in the city of Minneapolis.

Jacques Lemaire, the first coach of the Minnesota Wild, guided the team to 25 wins during the 2000 season and remained as the head coach for seven additional seasons. In Lemaire's third season, the Wild reached the **playoffs** for the first time. While there, the team made a surprising run to reach the Western Conference Finals before eventually being eliminated by the Anaheim Mighty Ducks.

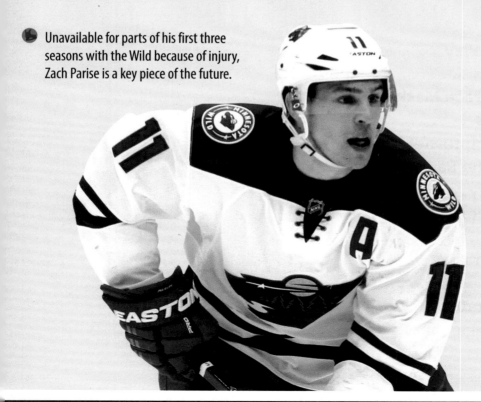

Unavailable for parts of his first three seasons with the Wild because of injury, Zach Parise is a key piece of the future.

In 2008, the Wild won its only division title, capturing the Northwest Division with 44 regular season victories, though the team did not win a playoff series that year. The Wild ended its nine-season playoff drought during the 2013–2014 postseason, defeating the Colorado Avalanche in seven games before being eliminated by the Chicago Blackhawks.

Center Mikko Koivu has only played for one NHL team, the Wild.

Minnesota Wild

Arena Xcel Energy Center

Division Central

Head Coach Michael Yeo

Location St. Paul, Minnesota

NHL Stanley Cup Titles None

Nicknames None

409 Sellouts in a Row

5 Playoff Appearances

3 Head Coaches

1 Division Title

History

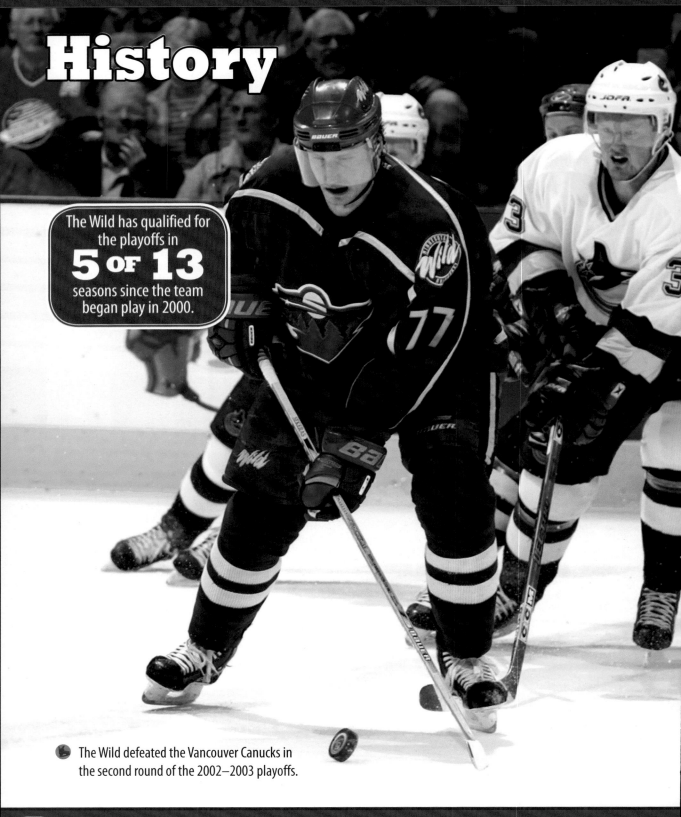

The Wild has qualified for the playoffs in **5 OF 13** seasons since the team began play in 2000.

The Wild defeated the Vancouver Canucks in the second round of the 2002–2003 playoffs.

Seven years after the North Stars left to play in Dallas, Texas, the Wild replaced them as the NHL's newest team Minnesota. Of the six proposed team names for the new NHL franchise, including Blue Ox, Freeze, Northern Lights, Voyage and White Bears, the Wild came out on top. The song "Born to be by the band Steppenwolf rang from the arena's speakers, signal the franchise's new name and new beginning.

Just three seasons after the team started to play, the Wild delighted fans by reaching the playoffs. After winning 42 reg season games, the Wild won the franchise's first two playoff during the 2002–2003 playoffs. Though the team's remarkal run ended one step shy of the Stanley Cup Final, that memc season reignited a proud hockey fan base in Minnesota.

After its exciting playoff run, the Wild continued the positive momentum, posting seven straight winning seasons. The te 48 victories during the 2006–2007 season remains a franchis best. Though the team has yet to capture the ultimate prize a Stanley Cup, the talented franchise hopes for more playoff appearances and a chance to someday hold a Stanley Cup.

In one of the greatest individual seasons in Wild history, Marian Gaborik scored 42 goals in 2007–2008.

The Arena

After 409 straight sold-out games, the Wild's first non-sellout in franchise history took place on September 23, 2010, in an exhibition game against the St. Louis Blues, almost 10 years after the Wild franchise began play.

The Xcel Energy Center is located In St. Paul, Minnesota. The arena welcomes approximately 1.7 million visitors each year to 150 different sporting and entertainment events. The "X," as the arena is nicknamed, has a list of accolades to go along with its many attendance records. In 2004, ESPN named the arena the second-best overall sports venue in the United States. In 2010, a Minnesota Wild game at the "X" was listed as the third-best arena experience in North America. The Twin Cities were selected as the hosting metropolis for the 2008 Republican National Convention, and the arena was chosen as the main venue.

As one of the largest arenas in the state, the Xcel Energy Center can hold around 18,000 fans for a hockey game. With free internet and multiple lounges where fans can eat and watch the hockey action, the arena makes every home game as comfortable as it is entertaining. Exclusive lounges, such as the NHL Alumni Lounge or the Treasure Island Ice Lodge, offer fans a chance to enjoy a wildly fun night, and potentially, a Wild victory.

The Xcel Energy Center hosted the Republican National Convention in 2008, where John McCain and Sarah Palin were nominated to run for president and vice president of the United States.

Where They Play

British Columbia

Alberta

CANADA

Saskatchewan

Manitoba

Ontario

7

4

3

14

Washington

Montana

North Dakota

Minnesota

Wisconsin

Oregon

Idaho

South Dakota

11

The Xcel Energy Center, St. Paul

8

Iowa

Wyoming

UNITED

Nebraska

Illinois

6

Nevada

STATES

Kansas

Missouri

Utah

Colorado

9

13

California

5

Arizona

New Mexico

Oklahoma

Arkansas

1

2

Pacific Ocean

MEXICO

Texas

10

Louisiana

Mis

Gulf of Mexico

WESTERN CONFERENCE

PACIFIC DIVISION

1 Anaheim Ducks
2 Arizona Coyotes
3 Calgary Flames
4 Edmonton Oilers
5 Los Angeles Kings
6 San Jose Sharks
7 Vancouver Canucks

CENTRAL DIVISION

8 Chicago Blackhawks
9 Colorado Avalanche
10 Dallas Stars
★ 11 Minnesota Wild
12 Nashville Predators
13 St. Louis Blues
14 Winnipeg Jets

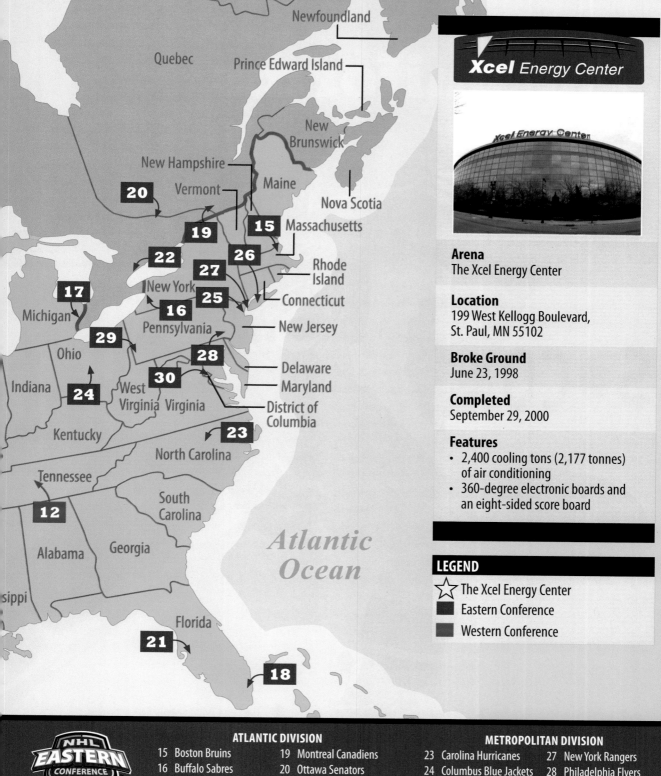

Xcel Energy Center

Arena
The Xcel Energy Center

Location
199 West Kellogg Boulevard,
St. Paul, MN 55102

Broke Ground
June 23, 1998

Completed
September 29, 2000

Features
- 2,400 cooling tons (2,177 tonnes) of air conditioning
- 360-degree electronic boards and an eight-sided score board

LEGEND
☆ The Xcel Energy Center
■ Eastern Conference
■ Western Conference

NHL EASTERN CONFERENCE

ATLANTIC DIVISION
15 Boston Bruins
16 Buffalo Sabres
17 Detroit Red Wings
18 Florida Panthers
19 Montreal Canadiens
20 Ottawa Senators
21 Tampa Bay Lightning
22 Toronto Maple Leafs

METROPOLITAN DIVISION
23 Carolina Hurricanes
24 Columbus Blue Jackets
25 New Jersey Devils
26 New York Islanders
27 New York Rangers
28 Philadelphia Flyers
29 Pittsburgh Penguins
30 Washington Capitals

The Uniforms

1 Upon entering the NHL, the Wild retired the number one, as a way of honoring their fans.

The color harvest gold can best be seen on the gloves Wild players wear.

HOME

The Minnesota Wild's team colors are forest green, iron range red, harvest gold, Minnesota wheat, and white. During home games, the team wears red jerseys with green arm stripes. At away games, players wear white jerseys with dark pants. In 2009, they added an alternative green jersey in addition to their traditional green and white jerseys.

The Wild **logo** is on the front of the home and away jerseys. The logo depicts both a forest landscape and the silhouette of a wild animal. The eye of the "Wild Animal" is the North Star, in tribute to the departed Minnesota North Stars.

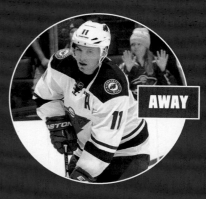

AWAY

The Wild logo does not appear anywhere on the alternative jerseys.

Helmets and Face Masks

1 The Total Pro Sports website ranked Josh Harding number one on its list of best goalie helmets of 2013–2014.

Niklas Backstrom sports some of the most striking goalie helmets in the league.

The Minnesota Wild helmets are forest green or white. On the road, players wear the white helmets. They wear green helmets in front of their home fans. During the 2012–2013 season, the Wild wore a commemorative "24/38" sticker on their helmets to honor Derek Boogaard and Pavol Demitra, two former Wild players who died unexpectedly during the summer before the season started.

Though most helmets look identical, goaltender helmets are much more decorative, as goalies are allowed to be creative with their designs. In the 2013–2014 season, the Wild used five different goaltenders. The most original design was displayed by former Wild goalie Ilya Bryzgalov, who decorated his helmet with drawings of Sonic the Hedgehog, a character from a famous video game. The helmet is Wild red and green, showing Sonic and his sidekicks in action.

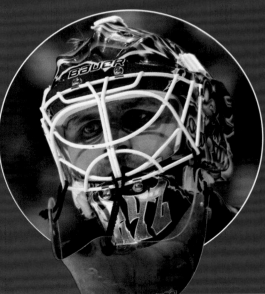

Despite very different helmet designs, Wild goalies tend to stick to the core team colors of forest green and iron range red.

The Coaches

3 The Minnesota Wild has had only three coaches in team history.

🌀 Mike Yeo is the youngest coach in the NHL.

The Minnesota Wild has not been quick to change coaches. The team's first coaching hire, Jacques Lemaire, was a consistent winner, who set the standard for the victories that followed. In fact, all head coaches of the Wild have had winning records while behind the bench in Minnesota.

JACQUES LEMAIRE Jacques Lemaire was the first coach of the Minnesota Wild. As a player, he won eight Stanley Cups. In 1984, he was inducted into the NHL Hall of Fame for his achievements on the ice. As a coach, Lemaire's 617 career wins rank him eighth in NHL history. Lemaire coached eight seasons for the Wild before being replaced by Todd Richards. Lemaire now works as a special assignment coach for the New Jersey Devils.

TODD RICHARDS Though Todd Richards only coached the team for two seasons, Richards guided the Wild to an overall winning record of 77-71-16 during his short stint in the Twin Cities. Richards quickly moved on to become the head coach of the Columbus Blue Jackets. The 2014–2015 season marked his fourth season in Ohio.

MIKE YEO Mike Yeo is the current coach of the Minnesota Wild. Although Yeo has less experience than some of his colleagues, he is a fiery competitor who can boast a winning record of 104-82-26. After Yeo's original three-year contract expired, the Wild re-signed Yeo to another three-year deal on May 31, 2014. The Wild front office believes Yeo is the right man to lead the young and talented Wild deep into the playoffs, and to capture Lord Stanley's Cup.

Fans and the Internet

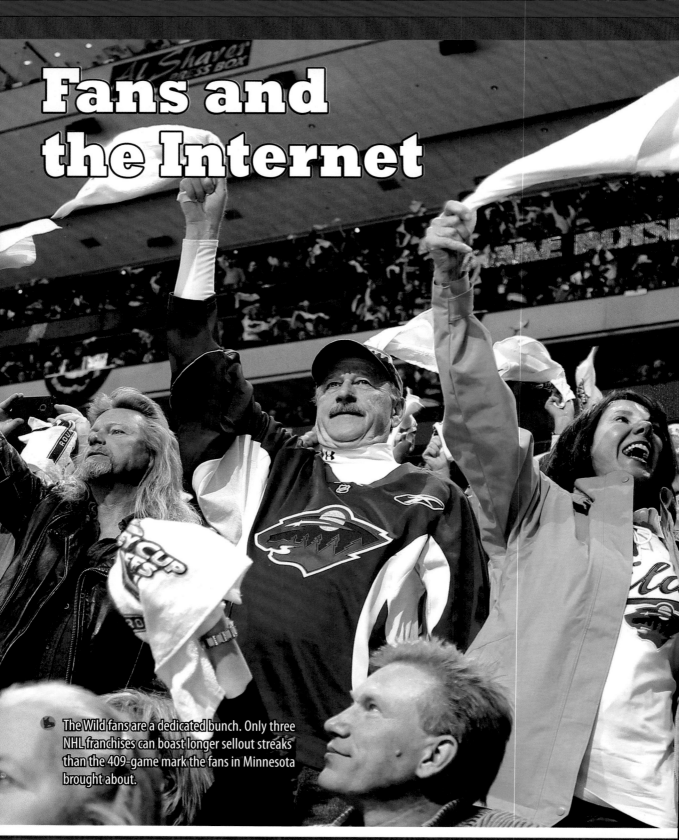

The Wild fans are a dedicated bunch. Only three NHL franchises can boast longer sellout streaks than the 409-game mark the fans in Minnesota brought about.

The Wild has its very own theme song, called "The Wild Anthem." Fans enthusiastically sing the anthem before games begin and during stoppages in play. The song was created during the 2000 season and has since become a source of pride for the Wild's fans.

Fans also gather online at popular Wild websites, especially the Wild's official NHL site, www.wild.nhl.com, a place for fans to buy tickets, view photos, create their own Wild accounts, and read the latest articles about their favorite players. The website includes individual player statistics and a historical section that details different Minnesota Wild team achievements. Popular Wild blogs include Hockey Wilderness, State of Hockey News, and Gone Puck Wild. These popular sites offer fans the opportunity to discuss and debate all things Minnesota Wild.

Signs
of a fan

#1 The Minnesota Wild Kids Club offers members free Wild gifts, such as lunch boxes, photos, stickers, and headphones. Kids also get invitations to exclusive arena events.

#2 Wild fans buy personal fan packs that include individual player cards and small magnetized game schedules for the refrigerator.

Legends of the Past

Many great players have suited up for the Wild. A few of them have become icons of the team and the city it represents.

Marian Gaborik

Marian Gaborik is a former Wild player who currently plays for the Los Angeles Kings. He started his NHL career with the Wild and spent eight seasons with the team until he joined the New York Rangers in 2009. Gaborik is a valuable player and a consistent offensive threat, though he often struggled with various injuries while in Minnesota. Gaborik was selected as an **All-Star** four times during his eight seasons with the Wild

Position: Right Wing
NHL Seasons: 14 (2000–Present)
Born: February 14, 1982, in Trencin, Czechoslovakia

Pierre-Marc Bouchard

Pierre-Marc Bouchard played for the Wild before moving on to play for the New York Islanders. During his career with the Wild, Bouchard became famous for his unique style and flair, including his famous "spin-o-rama" goal against the Edmonton Oilers. He is considered a high-risk, high-reward center who likes to take chances that other players will not normally even attempt. Bouchard recorded 347 points during 10 years with the Wild.

Position: Center
NHL Seasons: 11 (2002–2014)
Born: April 27, 1984, in Sherbrooke, Quebec, Canada

Brent Burns

Brent Burns is unique, both in personality and on the ice. He is rare in the fact that he has played both as a forward and a defenseman during his NHL career. Off the ice, his home is nicknamed the "Burns Zoo" because of his vast animal collection, which includes many types of snakes. Originally drafted by the Wild, he played seven seasons in Minnesota before joining the San Jose Sharks.

Position: Right Wing
NHL Seasons: 11
(2003–2014)
Born: March 9, 1985, in Ajax, Ontario, Canada

Andrew Brunette

Andrew Brunette has played for six teams in the NHL, including the Wild and the Colorado Avalanche. He has played more than 1,100 games. Brunette was signed by the Wild in 2008 as a **free agent**. With 119 goals, he is the third-leading goal scorer in the history of the franchise. After his retirement, Brunette became active with the Wild again as a hockey operations advisor. In his new role, he is in charge of scouting talented new players.

Position: Left Wing
NHL Seasons: 16 (1993–2012)
Born: August 24, 1973, in Sudbury, Ontario, Canada

Stars of Today

Today's Wild team is made up of many young, talented players who have proven that they are among the best in the league.

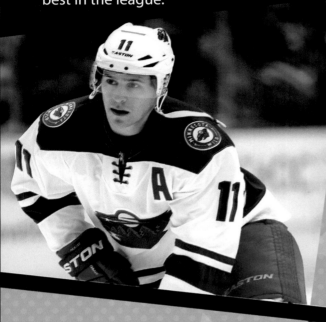

Zach Parise

When fans dream of seeing their team raise the Stanley Cup in Minnesota, much of that excitement stems from Zach Parise, a Minnesota-born player who is at the heart of the team's plans for the future. Parise played for the 2005, 2007, 2008, and 2010 U.S. Men's Olympic Ice Hockey Teams. He won a silver medal with his team in Vancouver at the 2010 Olympic Winter Games, further cementing his immense worth as a player. Slowed by injuries in all three of his seasons in Minnesota, Parise will need to prove he can stay healthy for the Wild. When available, his talent is off the charts.

Position: Left Wing
NHL Seasons: 10 (2005–Present)
Born: July 28, 1984, in Minneapolis, Minnesota, USA

Mikko Koivu

Mikko Koivu is the current captain of the Wild. He was also captain of the Finnish National Team in 2011 at the Men's World Ice Hockey Championships. Koivu is known for his loyalty, as he has only played for one team, the Wild. His dedication to remaining in Minnesota has endeared him to his fans. Koivu's brother, Saku Koivu, also played 18 seasons in the NHL. Though the brothers were originally nervous about competing against one another, they eventually found the experience to be rewarding.

Position: Center
NHL Seasons: 10 (2005–Present)
Born: March 12, 1983, in Turku, Finland

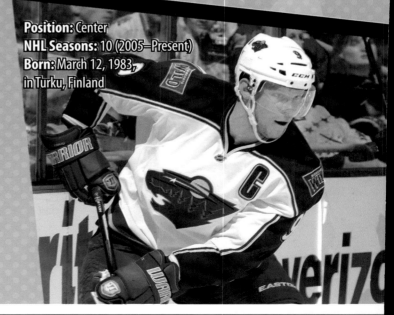

Ryan Suter

Ryan Suter has played for the Nashville Predators and the Wild during his time in the NHL. His father, Bob Suter, is famous for his role in the "Miracle on Ice" team that won the Olympic gold medal in 1980 in Lake Placid, New York. Ryan Suter, like his father, has also competed in the Olympics, both in 2010 and 2014, for Team USA. He is considered to be one of the best defensemen in the NHL. Suter hopes to join his father with his own gold medal and eventually one-up him with a Stanley Cup Championship.

Position: Defenseman
NHL Seasons: 10 (2005–Present)
Born: January 21, 1985, in Madison, Wisconsin, USA

Niklas Backstrom

Niklas Backstrom is one of the team's goaltenders. In 2006, Backstrom won the William Jennings Trophy for allowing the fewest number of goals that season. After backing up Manny Fernandez, Backstrom got his chance to play when Fernandez was injured, and led the NHL that season in **save percentage** and **goals against average**. For seven years, he started between the pipes in Minnesota and continues to see action there, though his game play has dropped considerably as the Wild continues to look for ways to keep Backstrom healthy and fresh in the net.

Position: Goaltender
NHL Seasons: 9 (2006–Present)
Born: February 13, 1978, in Helsinki, Finland

All-Time Records

83
Most Points in a Single Season
Marian Gaborik holds the team record for 83 points in a single season.

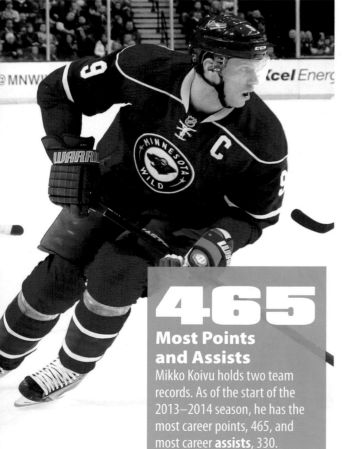

465
Most Points and Assists
Mikko Koivu holds two team records. As of the start of the 2013–2014 season, he has the most career points, 465, and most career **assists**, 330.

193
Most Wins
Niklas Backstrom owns a pair of team records. His 193 career wins and 37 victories in a single season are unmatched.

1,523
Most penalty minutes

Matt Johnson, a former Wild left winger, is infamous for the 1,523 penalty minutes he served during his career.

743
Most Games Played

Nick Schultz, a defenseman, leads the Wild with 743 games played. Mikko Koivu and Pierre-Marc Bouchard follow closely behind Schultz in this category.

Timeline

Throughout the team's history, the Minnesota Wild has had many memorable events that have become defining moments for the team and its fans.

2003
The Wild qualifies for the playoffs just three short seasons after its start in the NHL. The team reaches the Western Conference Finals before being defeated by the Anaheim Mighty Ducks.

2004
The season is canceled because of an NHL **lockout**, meaning no teams are able to play during that season. The Wild awaits another opportunity to take the ice and prove themselves.

| 1996 | 1998 | 2000 | 2002 | 2004 | 2006 |

In 2000, the Minnesota Wild is born. The team name was chosen over other candidates such as Blue Ox, Freeze, Northern Lights, Voyageurs, and White Bears.

2005
Despite a down year, Wild players Marian Gaborik and Brian Rolston respectively set new team records for most points and goals that season.

2006
The Wild signs a key pair of free agents, Kim Johnsson and Mark Parrish, in building a roster that can compete now and in the future.

2007

Niklas Backstrom becomes the main goaltender for the Wild. Behind his steady net play, the team claims its first division title.

The Future

Still a relatively young franchise, the Wild is certainly poised for a memorable future. First, the team will need to find consistent play from its goaltending group. Beyond that, the Wild will need some better luck with injuries. If players can remain healthy and defend their net, there is no question that the team has enough skilled players to bring a Stanley Cup to some of the most passionate fans in the league.

| 2008 | 2010 | 2012 | 2014 | 2016 | 2018 |

2009

Todd Richards is chosen as the new coach for the Wild after Jacques Lemaire resigns and returns to the New Jersey Devils.

In 2013, the Wild reaches the playoffs but is defeated by the Chicago Blackhawks, who would go on to win the Stanley Cup.

2011

Coach Todd Richards is replaced with current coach Mike Yeo. The fiery young coach directs the team back to the playoffs after just one season.

Write a Biography

Life Story

A person's life story can be the subject of a book. This kind of book is called a biography. Biographies often describe the lives of people who have achieved great success. These people may be alive today, or they may have lived many years ago. Reading a biography can help you learn more about a great person.

Get the Facts

Use this book, and research in the library and on the internet, to find out more about your favorite Wild. Learn as much about this player as you can. What position does he play? What are his statistics in important categories? Has he set any records? Also, be sure to write down key events in the person's life. What was his childhood like? What has he accomplished off the field? Is there anything else that makes this person special or unusual?

Use the Concept Web

A concept web is a useful research tool. Read the questions in the concept web on the following page. Answer the questions in your notebook. Your answers will help you write a biography.

Concept Web

Adulthood
- Where does this individual currently reside?
- Does he or she have a family?

Your Opinion
- What did you learn from the books you read in your research?
- Would you suggest these books to others?
- Was anything missing from these books?

Childhood
- Where and when was this person born?
- Describe his or her parents, siblings, and friends.
- Did this person grow up in unusual circumstances?

Accomplishments off the Field
- What is this person's life's work?
- Has he or she received awards or recognition for accomplishments?
- How have this person's accomplishments served others?

Write a Biography

Help and Obstacles
- Did this individual have a positive attitude?
- Did he or she receive help from others?
- Did this person have a mentor?
- Did this person face any hardships?
- If so, how were the hardships overcome?

Accomplishments on the Field
- What records does this person hold?
- What key games and plays have defined his career?
- What are his stats in categories important to his position?

Work and Preparation
- What was this person's education?
- What was his or her work experience?
- How does this person work?
- What is the process he or she uses?

Trivia Time

Take this quiz to test your knowledge of the Minnesota Wild. The answers are printed upside down under each question.

1 What year did the Wild first join the NHL?

A. 2000

2 Who is the current head coach of the Wild?

A. Mike Yeo

3 What is the name of the arena where the Minnesota Wild plays?

A. Xcel Energy Center

4 Who is the team's current and locally born left wing?

A. Zach Parise

5 What is the name of the Wild's main team song?

A. The Wild Anthem

6 Who was the first coach of the Minnesota Wild?

A. Jacques Lemaire

7 Which Finnish player won the Jennings Award for allowing the fewest goals in a single season?

A. Niklas Backstrom

8 What famous character was on Ilya Bryzgalov's goaltender helmet?

A. Sonic the Hedgehog

9 Which player's father was on the "Miracle on Ice" team in 1980?

A. Ryan Suter

Key Words

All-Star: a game made for the best-ranked players in the NHL that happens mid-season. A player can be named an All-Star and then be sent to play in this game.

assists: a statistic that is attributed to up to two players of the scoring team who shoot, pass, or deflect the puck toward the scoring teammate

franchise: a team that is a member of a professional sports league

free agent: a player who is allowed to play for a team without having a contract with a specific team

goals against average: a statistic that is the average of goals allowed per game by a goaltender

lockout: a lockout in the NHL takes place when the owners and players tangle in a labor dispute. The feud has grown bad enough in four instances that the owners have effectively "locked out" the players. The last lockout took place during the 2012–2013 season.

logo: a symbol that stands for a team or organization

playoffs: a series of games that occur after regular season play

save percentage: the rate at which a goalie stops shots being made toward his net by the opposing team

Index

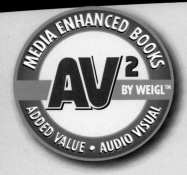

Log on to www.av2books.com

AV² by Weigl brings you media enhanced books that support active learning. Go to www.av2books.com, and enter the special code found on page 2 of this book. You will gain access to enriched and enhanced content that supplements and complements this book. Content includes video, audio, weblinks, quizzes, a slide show, and activities.

AV² Online Navigation

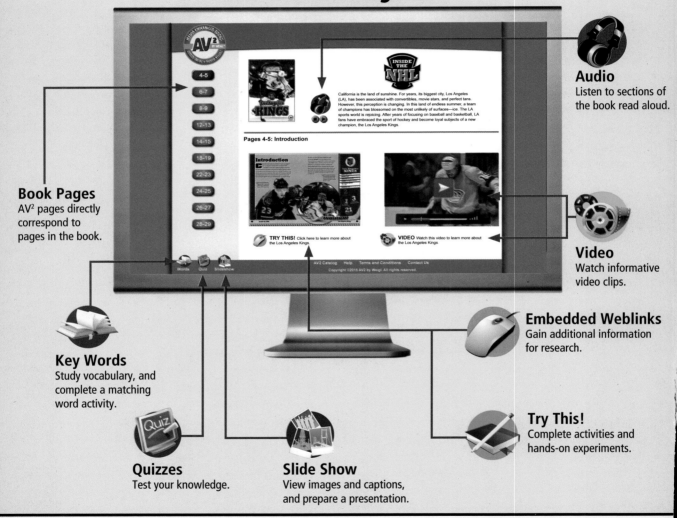

Book Pages
AV² pages directly correspond to pages in the book.

Audio
Listen to sections of the book read aloud.

Video
Watch informative video clips.

Embedded Weblinks
Gain additional information for research.

Try This!
Complete activities and hands-on experiments.

Key Words
Study vocabulary, and complete a matching word activity.

Quizzes
Test your knowledge.

Slide Show
View images and captions, and prepare a presentation.

AV² was built to bridge the gap between print and digital. We encourage you to tell us what you like and what you want to see in the future.

Sign up to be an AV² Ambassador at www.av2books.com/ambassador.

Due to the dynamic nature of the Internet, some of the URLs and activities provided as part of AV² by Weigl may have changed or ceased to exist. AV² by Weigl accepts no responsibility for any such changes. All media enhanced books are regularly monitored to update addresses and sites in a timely manner. Contact AV² by Weigl at 1-866-649-3445 or av2books@weigl.com with any questions, comments, or feedback.